T0047203

IT IS THE SEEING

By Renita Martin

Wildheart Press

ISBN 978-0-96630-973-7 (Print)
ISBN 978-1-66781-898-6 (eBook)

For Michelle

Acknowledgements

Thank you to God and my ancestors for holding, guiding, and gifting me with sight, compassion, and redemption. Mama, thank you for birthing me every day. Michelle Martin, you are my witness and heartbeat. Haley Bender, thank you for showing me my new self while being uniquely your own brilliant self. Thank you to Tia Juana Malone, my forf cuzin on my mama's side; David Bickham, who pushes me; Denise McDuffie Bentley for absolute love; Debra Mendes for the laughter; Nadine Jones for enduring friendship; Angelina Fiordellisi for believing; my cousins who affirm and love me; my aunts and uncles for being my best instructors; Ifé Franklin for being my place to laugh, cry, gossip, and create; Daniel Alexander Jones for seeing me; Sharon Bridgforth for creating family; Julie Rioux for making magic with me; Ramona Williams, my long-time confidant and inspiration; and Cousin Ruby Cannon, you loved me from the top of the show. Thank you to Ann Scales, Evelyn Moore, and Lisa Moore for your thoughtful editorial feedback during this process. Ekua Holmes, your gorgeous image perfectly articulates my words. Letta Neely, I love you, how we spiral.

Barbara, you define goodness. It is my joy to love you.

This book is offered in gracious memory of Laurie Carlos, Dr. Otrie B. Hickerson, Epiphana "Sylvia" Simon, Dorothy Owens Dixon, and Victoria Dixon.

Cover art *Menemsha* by Ekua Holmes
Edited by Letta Neely and Evelyn Moore

Table of Contents

let me scratch yo scalp

tell me
you ain't never had nobody scratch yo head
you ain't never had nobody
you ain't never had
you ain't never

you ain't
telling me
you don't know the soothe of mighty fingers
strolling through your Black woods
daring to love you cause you theirs

you don't say
you ain't never had
nobody tell you to
hold yo head still while
she gossiped –
"sho nuff? say she did?
she can't do nuthin with that lil fas gurl."

I wanna scratch yo scalp
grease yo soul
rub a little healing on yo kitchen/
put this love
on yo head since

you
tell me
you ain't
you ain't never
you ain't never had
you ain't never had nobody
you ain't never had nobody scratch yo scalp

Fire!

call me james brown while i dance on
the cum stained floor of your steamy
juke joint/
and let these legs be eyes
seeing rhythms
in shades of
1 - brown, 2 - red, 3 - bronze,
4 - yellow, 5, 6, 7, 8 Black toes
already in the water and we
burning up the floor, burning up
the roof, burning down this
house

burning til sage stick becomes fire and
this joint is smudged
with nothing else
but the smoke of the rhythm of color…

until there is nothing else
but us/here in this
charred slow drag called us/here/

The Forever Feast

Doubt is a steak knife slicing
You into baby bites

Don't be a morsel
Be the *flavor* -
The first and forever taste

Remain.

Long after the feast is finished

Novella

mama named her novella
which proved appropriate
since she was fatter than a short story and
shorter than a novel
she made you wonder if
Name made the woman
or did Woman make the name

they say novella drank herself to death was
drankin moonshine long fore
any body else even knew bout the stuff
but then, that ain't quite it, ain't quite when it started
novella never was quite right never had been right
since somebody stolt her doll baby back when she was nine
"matter of fact," most folk say,
"novella died long fore she stopped breathing."

she never had many words said
only what was necessary
stopped talking when necessary wore out
communicated mostly in punctuation
dot dot dot
dash
comma
stand up

"shit
well that's all i gots to say bout the matter."

period.

would leave you still talking
to her rocking chair on the porch,
close the screen,
be in her bed fore it stopped rocking

but she never did sleep
would wake up screaming, play some music,
drink some more try to sleep again
she thought too much bout too
many things
felt everything
said most time living in this world was
like bathing in a tub of acid.
said, "everybody gone burn, the bible say that,
just gotta figure out
if you gone do it from the outside in
or the inside out"

neighbors say her eyes was wide
open when they found her
next to the note that read,

"I didn't leave nuthin to nobody.
shit.
wasn't I enough?"

Free Thought

How do you enslave a man?
Dress him first.
Brand your name
On all his clothes.
Tell him he is naked
Without you.

Accessorize him.
Let him pick his own chains
Bedazzled with diamonds
Mined by his own siblings
Teach him to wear those chains
Even when you are not in the room.

Make him bite his tongue
Until it bleeds consent.

Remind him that he is better
Than the others,
The exception.
Never let him be the rule.

Tell him his thoughts are free -
Not purchased by greed for a steal,
Not paid for over and over and over again

By his mama, her mama, Medgar, Emmit, Philando,
Sandra, Breonna...

Teach him to smoke his grief,
Inhale, swallow, grin
As he licks his blunt-stained lips.
Give him a glass, watch him fill it with rage.
Drink, pour, drink, pour, drink poor
Regurgitate.

No need to stand in the sizzling sun, whip in hand,
For he can no longer bear sunlight.
Bring him into the big house.
Watch him become
At once the whip and the slave.

See him cowering in the mirror?
Whispering to his fractured soul
"You are your own master.
You, your own slave."

the choir

gospel choir was full of us doing

more talking than singing
in vivid declarations talking to prove -
despite whispered rumors

that leaped outside crescendos – we

were the sexual that is Godly

gospel choir was full of us creating secret duets that
drowned in the blood of jesus,
singing in loud silent fear of living alone,
dying unheard,
performing a symphony of fantasies
to make us alright

Raindrop

in the absence of familiar
she called her raindrop
because her eyes dripped
rainbow moist dew
into the fire of her thighs
those hips at once made and
devastated her day
always stirring like tomorrow
just a few steps from reach

she thought of clothespins
on her nipples wanted clothespins/on her nipples/wanted
raindrop to hang laundry from her peak

she had seen her uncle
throw watermelon to the earth
laugh wild fold his hands
scoop red cloud from the ground
exclaim, "goddamn it's good!"
she wanted cause to say, "goddamn
it's good!"
as raindrop's vine writhed below her
patch

she wanted to throw raindrop down
watch her burst cup her hands
and eat
while raindrop exclaimed,
"this juice will stain"

trans/formation

there is room for me
blood i ain't
gon dip see

cause the
world is outside this box
i was shipped here in so

push on baby cause i'm
bout ta ride out this metal tugging at my ankles i am not
afraid of falling anymore
have learned to propel the galaxies swim the stars
be my destination!

I am making motion out of dust
sunshine outta shade
fire in the middle of this hurricane

i been here
gon be here alight!

Peculiar Wars

I guess every generation got they own peculiar war ta fight. I wasn't nuthin but a baby when I got married. So happy ta be out that lil bitty house. Wife of a preacher! Was so used to fittin myself up in tight spaces, all I wanted was a shotgun house. Mr. Griffin say, "Not for my wife, not no shotgun house." Been in this big white house by the side of the road ever since. And Lawd knows I needed it. Raised thirteen chillen and mo grandchillen than I can count.

And never coulda seent the wars that would come they way.

My baby boy, Claude come runnin up in the house one day talkin bout he was gonna march wit them civil righters. Now, me and Mr. Griffin hadn't never been scared of no white folk. But, we hadn't never had no real need to be round em. Specially marchin, wit our backs to them, they guns, and they mangy dogs.

And it's somethin holy bout birthin babies, so holy that even if you done armed em and you know the war they goin out ta fight is righteous, you'd lay yo own tired Black flesh on steamy, slick roads fore you let em go out dere… be every hound dog's mangled milkbone fore you let them white folk turn em on yo babies.

And jes when some folk thought the war had ended. The bullets started flyin again.

But this war is got ta be the most peculiar one yet. Cause my grandbaby, Darryl, didn't come to me so's I could tell him not ta go out dere. And even if he had, me telling him not ta go wouldna done no good. Cause the war ain't out there no mo.

This peculiar war got my grandbabies runnin in every direction tryna find some peace. When Darryl got kilt, his sister, Re Re couldn't sit still. She say them bullets and drugs is like them ee-lectric brooms they got out now. Say they might suck huh up next.

So, she moved up north. Outta that blue choir robe, out the church, put some little nappy, nubby balls in huh head, and bloomed right on out to Boston. Out the closet (like they say on Oprah), outta dem nice girdles I got huh to keep huh figure. Replaced them with no bra. Talkin bout bras was oppressive. Now, I ain't never seen no woman — feminist or not — who didn't droop. I told huh by the time she git thirty, she was gonna be milking huh toes.

She tell me ain't no different for Black folks up there. I told her I knowed that. If you finds that a apple is rotten on one side, biting the other side of the same apple ain't gonna brang you the fresh taste ya lookin fa.

I asked huh, "Why you gotta tell everybody what you is? You know they killin up the gays." She say she gotta be. I tole huh — it's a whole lotta ways ta be, and dead is one of em. She jes say, "It's a whole lotta ways ta be dead."

It All Started with Backtalk

My first word was
"Ain't."

The request, innocent enough -
Met a rugged resistance
That still refuses to buckle

"You better put these on.
Right now!"

I would be free
Not bound
By patent leather
And hurt feet
I dug in my heels, and
Flat-out refused.

Poor Mama's heart stumbled.
"So, this is how it's gon be?"
We stared.
Exhausted and
Stifling a giggle,
Mama dropped the shoe, collapsed.

"Well.
I'm gonna tell your daddy when he gets home."

My second word was
"So."

Stuck

you slid into my honey too fast
it seems i don't know whether
to keep running like a stray bullet
or stay and conceive
of loving you sweet
in warm, sacred, uncomplicated spaces

you came
lining my lips with honey
too fast, i'm stuck
want you in my routine
want to be in your honey
all the time

to make love with you in and out of bed
to breed worlds with you
harmonize smooth in time
slide sweet, baby, slide on into my honey

cherry preserves

perhaps i did
just fall off the cherry tree
i am a bit stiff and bruised
there is a fresh scar
that runs clear to the pit

if i did
just fall off
it ain't right to pull out the mason jar
just because i'm too bruised to eat
too sweet to throw away

you wanna let me congeal
til your peanut butter runs out
so you can jam me
between two slices of your wonderbread
when you know
that ain't right
even if i did fall in your back yard.

off my heart

the old folks would say
i need to ask the lord to take you off my heart. and i
have asked the lord
to not ask me nuthin else about you.
stilled in this veil of mourning.
i keep telling the lord
i ain't got nuthin else to say.
period.

but, She won't listen She
just keeps askin…

i answer:
in this poem, only,
can i run bare-chested to the bosom of earth,
fingernails buried in the cum
of a thousand dews i can find rest –
come, just hold, hold, hold…

sometimes this moan
is the only place i can fly,
de-winged in spirit without you,
i am trying to learn to levitate from this seductive pit, this dull
gray catastrophic summoning of death.
to find a new spelling of mourning
where the "r" suddenly reverses like a rebellious stallion
trampling over the "u"
like it has been this way long enough.

to see, like a baptized ancestor,

baptized into the soft black womb of spirit world. to see

a light so gentle

it is a subtle kiss on my barren back. to smell

a day so exquisite

it is a calm enema moving the bile of grief out of this

wounded shrine.

to see/ without you/

a sanctified dance in the wilderness. to

smell sunlight

on my upper lip.

This Ole Building

With suga diabetes
Slidin' 'cross this ole building
Like issa bow
And I is the fiddle,
I cain't do much more than sit here
Watchin' the same shows

My grandbabies wanna to get me a smart TV
But the picture ain't gon be no brighter
Justice? A picture tube that blowed out
Long 'fore the warranty was up
And America still won't gimme my money back

up north

pathos sways differently in the north
does not cling tight to Black necks while
cutting deep into oak trees

pathos moves swiftly through northern streets rolls
gently off political tongues
clings tight to trained blue boys
carelessly spraying the dark

Word

Word is

indistinguishable

from touch

The Race

Death is a toothless grin

At each corner
Of our course.
We stand
Trying to recall Freedom's spell

On cement slabs in this cold hell
Severed fingers lie still tangled
While we stand and try to recall her spell

In my dreams we rise
Naked in recollection, cloaked in possibility

We dance and recall her spell

I am awakened by delighted children
Who throw chants and giggles into
Cement cauldrons
We build new worlds
Groove here, recall her spell

the crosswalk

"hit me, muthahfuckah!"
is the sound that follows the screech that
follows the truth, that is,
"i ain't got nuthin to lose"

"i ain't got nuthin to lose"
is the song maybe rap or jazz
or an embryonic gospel blues tune
that ain't even been wrote yet was written before
it replaced the power of stop lights on crowded streets

"i ain't got nuthin to lose"
is the call and response
to a world tailored to wrap itself
around us each and each alone
that even from its suffocating embrace
resonates one dim song
"i ain't got nuthin to lose"

it is the seeing

there was the blood
the darkness the pavement
the us
fugitives running the always barefoot and bloody run away
from things we did not know.

mama was crying then was
always crying then
when tears were heavy enough to draw blood then
when we ran and
could not stop
even though her tears made our feet bleed her
fears made our noses bleed

this time it was the helicopters
she saw above our hood before
they arrived
and declared they were coming
she declared they were coming

when her moss covered black temple is dragged from
these muddy waters
they will not say she went crazy before then that
she spent the rest of her life there between crazy
and dead there
they will not say that she lived through all
kinds of people's rights movements
yet here was always lynching season for her — poor,
black, woman, crazy

drowning in the blood, the darkness, the pavement where
there were sewer rats who nibbled
at the fingers of her brain and devoured her
children's breakfast food
she almost killed us trying to kill them did
not sleep then.
i do not sleep now watching for sewer rats
to come drink from the mucous of this condition.

perhaps they will say that crazy is elegant some
kind of pure response
to the inelegant that is our lives
perhaps they will lie and say they treated her like elegance polished
her shit-stained ass when she was afraid
to go to the bathroom
washed and held her when they found her again
covered in piss hair uncombed because
the comb was a nuclear weapon sent her by the CIA

it is the seeing that drives you mad it is
the seeing things appear then
disappear that might make you bleed

and she saw the helicopters and
declared they were coming
and
declared
they
were coming;

For Abner Louima

...started August 8, 2000
Still editing...

4:40 A.M.

hope is a trickster
holding a bullet-torn wallet
full of red, white, and blue promises
boasting a blood-stained smirk;

hope is forgetful,
well-intended, remnant;

hope cannot see
that quiet is a hologram,
smiles are warnings,
and even rainbows shed blood
sometimes;

for the spirits of miscarried lives

where are the keys to the kingdom? the
kingdom being your life being
oh standing at the door and i wanna come in

i'm tired of calling you up in services holding you up like
*that precious ember

that was
that patent leather shoe
that was
all that little girl's mama had left
in Birmingham one day after Sunday school.

they say you won't wear this shoe
again, say this time
it ain't the shoe that's melted.
it's you.
i can't take this again
can't take this again
can't do another miscarried life

folks sang that Sunday in Birmingham
for that shoe levitating like the fiery chords of
some glad morning when this life is over i'll fly   away

and it must be something to bust out with a song anywhere you be
to sing a love song with smoke in your soul
to let a blues song hold you
while you holding the shoe

cause you got salve to rub on burns
but you ain't got the foot

will one of y'all sing us a balm sing
a sanctified healing prayer sing
these bodies a mantra

sing up a foot in this here shoe i'm holding sing
up the keys to the kingdom,
Lawd, i'm standing at the door
and i wanna come in.

Where Are the Keys to the Kingdom? by Reverend Herbert Brewster
as sung by Sweet Honey in the Rock
Some Glad Morning (I'll Fly Away), Albert E. Brumley, 1932

Communion

St Luke 22:19

And he took bread, and gave thanks, and brake it, and gave onto them, saying, "This is my body which is given for you: this do in remembrance of me."

Fannie Lou rustles through leaves,
Settles at the root of my soul
And it has come to pass
That her beckoning is virtuous communion,
As I drink remembrance, I become her dream
A glorious reckoning, a hallelujah march
That will not stop

North Star

They will never say
I stomped loudly and unafraid
Steadily pounding Freedom's beat
Into the righteous flame of infinity

In fact, those who care enough
Have to often ask,
"What did you say?"
See, war has mangled my vocal cords

Left me whispering, dizzy, fumbling for breath -
An eternal toddler
Well acquainted
With the consequence of dissent

But they will never say
I did not try.
Tiptoeing like Harriet
Through the slithering light of night
Terrified, but here!
Rousing you gently, gifting you
With the one thing
I know for sure.

It is time.
Run! Now!
Towards that blazing star called Love

The Ride

I remember the day the training wheels came off.
How life accelerated as I reached up.
"Steady me, Ma,
Don't let me fall."

Today, life's training wheels have evaporated
And I don't know if my brakes are working,
Am I steering in the right direction?
Still, Mama trusts me, hangs tight for the ride.

She reaches up, grabs both my hands.
Arms around my waist,
She waits for me to stand her up,
Steady her,
Expects me to hold her up.

I pray her to the toilet,
Balance her on one hip,
Grab the tissue.
How I long for training wheels as I wipe.

She wobbles, pleading,
"Don't let me fall,"
"I won't."

My promise is almost a lie.
But I try
Even though I don't know
How long I can hold her.

I wonder if she felt this insufficient
Watching as I rolled away struggling
To steady myself
Confident that she would catch me before the pavement did.

The training wheels are gone,
The ride shorter – to the toilet, kitchen table, to bed.
I pedal, uncertain
As she grabs me firmly
Holds on, trusting

Peaches

Sometimes i be crying a little girl Bible story song like they be sangin in church. But i be crying. When i gets real scared and i can't even be big for my little brother no mo he just balls up in a little bitty rolly polly ball. If i kicks him hard enough he will roll on out of my bedroom. Stop keeping up all that wet racket. But i don't kicks him cause i love him — the very same reason my daddy do kick my mama.

My mama be sayin, "Why don't you pick on somebody yo own size." But she bigger than him, yellow like a peach gettin ready to be preserved. And bigger than him. But she can't fight like him. I thank it cause she don't be seeing the kind of thangs he be seeing. He say he have to fight demons every day. I don't thank my mama ever fought no demons so she probly ain't got that much strength bout herself. But my daddy, he be fighting demons. Outside when it be a tornado, or sometimes just thunder, he wanna fight. Be saying, "Come on big storm, you wants to dance?"

Me, myself, i ain't never seen no thunder dance. But my daddy, he be cuttin a jig with thunder like it is my mama. He be standing out there swingin my mama's Jack Daniels he be done drunk up fore she get home. He breaks the bottle off at the bottom and be cutting the wind.

One time i asked him, "Daddy, how come you can see thunder dancing and we can't?" He say our eyes ain't growed big enough yet. I don't know if i wants my eyes to grow no mo.

between us

these days words peek like fugitives
from wooded spaces
afraid to come out afraid to
say our well is
drying afraid to say
there is water somewhere afraid
to see what we must do to get
there
afraid that water does run uphill

there are ways they say of fighting this pharmaceutical
suspensions to ease the rumbling in your house
if you can pay again there are ways to die tomorrow

but who will speak of the final way of it all? a band-
aid's teeth can never clench a bullet long enough for
you to heal
who will say that the house
will still fall if the bullets don't stop

you did not want to go to the place of your birth in the
end "the house needs
fixing there is not enough room
for me and i am afraid afraid to
hear that
how i lived is why i cannot
afraid to want to stay under the blanket
        of my blazing delusions until

34

i can go because where i am is too cold
afraid to know finally
my fever is mild next to theirs"

now you speak to me in raspy dreams the
fear you did not divine was exile you tell
me they fix you
soup full of corn and okra and your father's spit you tell
me you don't like okra
that your mother keeps bringing the soup without
words while your grandfather prays tells you to
ask the lord
to pardon your being

you tell me the house is still falling but
to call again
"maybe i can get to the phone before they do. ring
once hang up call again," i say "okay"

i thought my songbook was full of
notes for all occasions
still there is no time
signature to dance them to
the place where i am family too

so i place two copper pennies
on each corner of my soul to bring wealth to these
days too short… too cold to be over this soon

and wait
for raspy dreams
for somebody's words to come out of hiding to
hear you say "it was a miracle but they finally
fixed the house"
to hear that water does run uphill and
everybody is ready to climb

show me the poem

somehow we are continuously carving. the naked gash
we thought was narrative seems to keep oozing
new language

even here,
where words struggle
to squeeze into our tiny bed

especially now. when
i thought i had exposed everything. heard it all.

i need more want to
read
the sweet, raw, wounded poem not written
in your book

We Blink

Be it 90 years or 90 seconds
Life is always
A vibrant flash through
That tiny town with no stop signs
You blink and you've missed it

But time can't mess with meaning
Meaning eclipses time every time
Is the sole thing that is significant

How love shapes the left side of your lip
Glistens from your right eye
How my breath chases itself
Every time you sprout into bloom

What you mean to me is specific
Like the laugh that spills from your head
Slung all the way back

We are why we drove through that tiny town
In the first place

We are our destination

dudley square

sun ran naked down the edges
of our backs climbed between skin and tank top bade
us smile even though the bus was late

one kid turned his music
all the way down locked arms with an old lady
strolled up the slender steps searching for
a place to seat her
the dyke in the third seat to the right stood up extended
her space thinking
"yes. we are all good kin folk"

even the junkie in the back
put his thang in his pants got on
deciding out loud
"i'ma piss downtown today"

we set in
made the 49 our home
hung rhythms on
the windows and
settled for the ride downtown

sun drew prisms on
our head wraps skipped cross baseball caps turned back we
looked up headed downtown.
no one
no one looked back
no one saw you cowered between street post and curb praying

perhaps for a place
aplacetolaydownyourbody
a place to lay down
no one knew you were that tired

when the bus rolled
sun screamed.
yo mama sat straight up from her sleep sat
up straight in bed called
15 hundred miles "baby, this is mama. call me, soon as you
get home.
i just had a terrible dream."

if we had seen you
lipstick smeared up angled
round your cheekbone
the railroads in the bend of your arms
what eyes narrate when dreams become gum
stuck
on the bottom of men's shoes

had we seen you

we would have stopped
put   some   chaka   on

showed you sun
showed you
sunbendingdown
to hold you.

Race to Run

Done with waiting,
No I won't take a number

My soul is sick and tired
Of pacing the floor at night,
I wonder
If it was you holding your breath
Every time your baby leaves
You waiting by the window to see
If she could breathe
Would you sing of how soon
We will overcome
Soon thy will be done
Soon as my savior come
Then I'm gon get me some?
Stand up!
And start building heaven right here.
I'm gonna see my God's face.

Did you think this gospel song would soothe you
Hear me singing bout a day
When love would finally move you?
You can call me love
Cause I'm done deliberating
Call me sick call me contagious
Just don't call me
Complacency
Is overrated

You think you made it
Think you are the exception
Steppin' Fetchin' never guessing that you
Might be the lesson
Stand up and start building heaven right here.

The Storm

for Sekou Sundiata

You darted the threshold, chimed "Honey,
I'm Home!"
God jumped up, twirled her skirt flamenco style
Stomped so loud the angels came stumbling out
Oshun lifted the top off the collard greens

"It's 5:47 in the morning!
Just 15 more minutes, please, Lord.
And why you cooking dinner before daybreak?" God
grinned,
"Sekou is home!"

born again

just when you thought the days of anonymous love were
over
she finds you at the after party in the corner of your room
huddled across the lover
you vowed to leave years ago
she grabs the mirror, blows!
leaves your lover helpless, spread out across the floor

you remember that last night
even earlier today
you would have chased your love
searched on your knees, straw in hand
crawling til you sucked up each grain

but this new passion is thick
when her lips curl up you forget
the finely chopped wife beater
you have been married to for so long

you ask her her name here
she gives you one hand
the other she runs across your stomach and
just for now
you
don't hate your stomach anymore
your form feels brilliant
your water descends
she leads you to bed loves you/slowly you

remember how to get home from here
when you awake you
don't want a cigarette
you just want her to show you that place she
found last night
the one
that upon touch sang out your name

she does
just before pushing her head all the way in
shoulders/ follow/ torso/enters
her legs are dangling from your pussy
you swallow her whole

"hey, you" you yell
"what you doing in there?"
you think
"whatever it is, it feels good"

water gushes past your hands
you have never come like this
and at this moment
you know her name
it is the same one that was yours before
you met fear handed him your dreams in exchange
for sleep
you shout "freedom?!
um freedom.
yes!
freedom done crawled up my pussy
and stayed."

Black Church

Hands baptized
in your pulpous religion,
the misty four-cornered wall of your raging, i am
congenitally immaculate

To give you this offering -
this sanctified red cave
washed and spread out
like the gentle Rose of Sharon, sweet and unconditional.

You showed me to see but Holy in your eyes,
miracles in a village thought to be extinct; your
tongue, precise splashes
ancestral libation on my volcanic ground;
your lips a silky waterfall in the middle of a desert

My rising nipples nestle in
the heat of your hair
as woolly as holy as the Lamb's
while medicinal hands,
ancient yet futuristic, hover.

I do dance in your arms. A holy dance
inside your throbbing edifice i dance
i dance
first giving honor to God, to the ancestors,
the spirits, to the pastor
and the waiting congregation

i dance in the sanctuary of you.

Seeing

Kinda like I woke up being everywhere
Kinda like I woke up feeling everything
Kinda like the puzzle pieces in the air
All lined up

Kinda like when you've been sleeping
Underneath the weight of the dreams
You've been keeping
Raise your head up
See the sun creeping
She taps you on the shoulder
Says, "Come along with me."

Kinda like I woke up being everywhere
Kinda like I woke up feeling everything
Kinda like the puzzle pieces in the air
All lined up

Kinda like how rain on a steamy day
Always serves to dry my fears away
Kinda like how the old folks used to say,
"Doubt can't stay where doubt can't find a place."

Kinda like I woke up being everywhere
Kinda like I woke up feeling everything
Kinda like the puzzle pieces in my head
All lined up

how ghetto gurl rose up

man! dis party was like off
the fuckin chain!
it wadn't nuthin but women there and
i'm like buggin
cause i ain't never been to no shit like this and
we was jes talkin you know
bout the hood and how we gon raise up

and at firs
i was like scared to talk cause
these bitches i'm sittin up here wit is bad and
i'm like "these hoes up in here
is deep, what i got ta say?" but then, i was
like, "fuck dis." i was all like, "what we
need is a black superhero" and they was
like, "yeah!"
den it wuz like the bionic woman up
in dat muthafuckah

dis lady, harriet was like "here, you can have my feet." now,
this bitch got some tough ass feet
she don been runnin through swamps
and rivers an shit, an ole as she look, them feets is
fast and tough and strong
as a muthafucka
den flo joe was like, "here take my legs."
i was like, "ah, naw! flo joe giving me the legs!"

and we all know every black superwoman got ta
have some ass. nuthin to it.

chaka was right there ta "tell me somethin good" i said
"chaka, you still need yo shit, girl."
chaka say, "naw, baby, i got enough ta go around."

this cleavage right here, dorothy dandridge.
i didn't even know who she was
til she walked up in the party and,
girl, you coulda heard a flea fart
i was all like, "who the fuck is that?"

all dese muscles and shit, all dis shit minez. ain't no
muthafuckah gon roll up on me dat i cain't push up
off me and i was all like
"y'all some pretty bitches, but i'ma keep my face, too"
cause it done took me a long time ta git use ta dis muthahfuckah.

dis lady, rosalind cash, was like,
"here, hold my quaff til i git back

and that'z how ghetto gurl rose up
and i ain't got time ta be changin in no muhfuckin phone boof what you
see is what you git

i got my celly
and you know the number, boo.

These Hands

Once upon a place
In a time far away
There stood a sister
In the darkness
With a pocket full of clay

She looked around
Looked around
Looked around
And she said
I'll make me a world
And I'll make it out of clay

She made a poet
Made a prophet
Made the stars
Made em sparkle
Made the sun
Made the moon

Fore you know it
We was walking
We was loving
We was giving
We'd get up
In the morning
Get up
With just one mission

What can I make today?
What can I make today?
What can I make today?
With these hands?

Once upon a place
In a time not too far away
We are all made brand new
We are all we again
We be the stars
Made from the darkness
We be the moon
Can't we see how we sparkle?

Now come the time
For the poet
For the prophet
For the earth
For the water
Keep on walking
Keep on giving
Keep on working
Keep on living
Get up in the morning
Get up
With just one mission

What can I make today?
What can I make today?
What can I make today?
With these hands?